Wreaths

Wreaths

FRESH, FORAGED & DRIED
FLORAL ARRANGEMENTS

Katie Smyth & Terri Chandler

Photography by Kristin Perers

Hardie Grant

QUADRILLE

To Paddy and Mike,
long may your
patience last x

Publishing Director Sarah Lavelle
Editor Harriet Butt
Creative Director Helen Lewis
Design and Art Direction Gemma Hayden
Photographer Kristin Perers
Prop Stylist Linda Berlin
Styling Katie Smyth & Terri Chandler
Production Director Vincent Smith
Production Controller Jessica Otway

Published in 2018 by Quadrille,
an imprint of Hardie Grant Publishing

Quadrille
52–54 Southwark Street
London SE1 1UN
quadrille.com

The moral rights of the authors have been asserted.

Text © Katie Smyth & Terri Chandler 2018
Photography © Kristin Perers 2018
Design © Quadrille Publishing 2018

ISBN 978 1 78713 120 0

Reprinted in 2018 (twice), 2019 (twice)
10 9 8 7 6 5

Printed in China

Contents

Introduction

CREATE SOMETHING FROM A FEW SIMPLE STEPS

Crafts using natural materials are having a bit of a moment. For the first time in years, it feels like people are foraging again for food and plant life to bring indoors. Nurturing that connection with the world around us and its changing seasons is important to us, and we want to encourage you to experience this too. Challenging yourself to make something out of a few stems you gathered while out for a walk, or from your garden, brings such satisfaction and a little bit of nature's beauty into your home.

Taking time out to create something for yourself is the most rewarding feeling. So rewarding that we have made it our lives! We were stuck in jobs that were making us feel a little bit sad, especially when setting the alarm every evening. Now when the alarm goes off (usually about 4am) we are giddy to get going (okay the giddiness might come a few hours later). Being around nature really does make you feel wonderful.

Over the last few years we have been lucky enough to travel for work and one of the things that we kept spotting in countries around the world were wreaths. They come in all sizes and materials, and they are used to mark a wide range of occasions, and with many different meanings. We have seen garlic-donned wreaths above the doorways of homes on Greek islands to welcome in the first day of May, wildflower wreaths in Scandinavia to signal midsummer, and in America the whole nation

is speckled with flamboyant door wreaths to celebrate Thanksgiving.

A wreath can be a wonderful gift, a warm welcome or a beautiful wall decoration. There are so many ways that wreaths, along with wall hangings, can be incorporated into your home.

Making something with meaning has always been really important to us. This is why we love the language of flowers and are always trying to convey a subtle message through everything we create. When we make a wreath for a wedding, for example, we always fill it with flowers that symbolise 'everlasting love'. You may like to take a similar approach with some of your wreaths, especially those for special occasions. You can find lots of information about the language of flowers on the Internet.

We love the thought of people going out to forage and making their very own beautiful creations which will be all so different depending on what part of the world they are from. We would be so happy to see some of your own creations!

Terri and Katie. Worm x

How to use this book

THERE ARE NO RULES

All the projects in this book are relatively straightforward. Have a look at the picture of each one; if it looks simple to make, then it probably is. Those that are bigger and appear more complicated may take longer to make and need more materials, but nothing in this book is very difficult when you are equipped with the right skills and techniques.

Please use our directions simply as guidelines. What we love most about these kinds of projects is that they are instinctive and natural; they will look completely different depending on the materials used and the creativity of the person making them.

When we host workshops, we often do a quick demonstration first so that our clients understand the making process. We then leave them to their own devices, and that is when we really see their personalities shine through. Some are neat and intricate, others brilliantly chaotic and wild. So try to go with what comes naturally to you and not just what you see in the picture.

We have tried to make the methods and materials in this book as accessible as possible. Some are not necessarily those used in traditional floristry, but this is how we make all of these projects ourselves. They also show how you can use shapes and materials that you may already have in your own home or garden to make something really personal and beautiful. Trust your instincts: if you are inspired to use a different material or method then go with it. There are no hard and fast rules to wreath making.

In the following section, we have included instructions on how to make a basic wreath using plant vine. Once you have mastered this, then you already have the beginning of many of the projects in the book. We also explain how to prepare floral foam, and give guidelines on using floristry wires.

We have tried, where possible, to include measurements and quantities in the projects, but again these are only guidelines. We encourage you to trust your own taste and judgement when collecting plant materials for a wreath and the amount to gather, and have confidence in your vision of how you would like your finished piece to look.

Many of the materials you need for making wreaths can be found in floristry supplies retailers, craft or hardware shops; most of the others you will find in nature.

Equipment

FROM TOP TO BOTTOM:

CALICO
We use calico or Irish linen to make hangers for many of our wreaths and mobiles. You can buy them by the metre/yard from your local haberdashery and cut them into strips. Calico is the cheaper of the two, but Irish linen is lovely to handle and comes in lots of beautiful shades.

DRESSMAKING SCISSORS
We have learned how important it is to use the correct scissors for the task at hand. Florist's scissors will ruin fabric, so dressmaking scissors are a must if you are cutting cloth.

CLEAR THREAD
Available from most craft or hardware shops, this comes in different thicknesses. It is good to have a really fine thread along with a thicker, stronger one that can take a bit of weight.

FLORIST'S SCISSORS
These are strong enough to cut woody stems as well as soft stems. Try to keep them dry so that they don't start to rust and become stiff.

ROLL OF TWINE
Always handy. Standard twine is often made from jute, a plant fibre, which gives it a rough texture and a natural, light brown colour that works well in most wreaths. You can also buy twine in different colours, which is useful if you need it to be camouflaged!

RUSTIC WIRE
This 18-gauge, heavy-duty, decorative wire is covered in a natural fibre, such as jute or ramie, and comes on a roll. It is great to use as a natural-looking base for garlanding.

BONSAI SCISSORS
These are really good for small, intricate cutting, getting into little gaps and for neatening up a project when it is finished.

SECATEURS
For cutting really thick woody stems and small branches – especially handy when out foraging.

GREEN FLORIST'S TAPE
This stuff is amazing. A self-adhesive tape, it doesn't feel sticky, yet when you stretch it and wrap it around itself the tape bonds and is waterproof too.

WIRE CUTTERS
Essential for cutting wire, and to avoid ruining your scissors trying to cut metal. When using wire cutters, be sure to always cut the wire away from you so that it won't accidentally fly into someone's eye!

BINDING WIRE
Also known as florist's or reel wire, this soft steel wire comes on a roll and is great for garlanding and many other tasks. Binding wire

continued on page 16...

Equipment

CONTINUED...

generally comes as standard in 24 gauge, which is a good gauge for wreath making, although other gauges are available (the gauge refers to thickness and strength of the wire, the lower the figure, the thicker and stronger the wire, so 24-gauge wire is finer than 18-gauge wire).

STUB WIRE
Available in bundles in pre-cut lengths, this thick green-coated wire is used to support stems or to wire on flowers. It is widely sold in 22-gauge, but other gauges are available.

ROSE WIRE
The finest wire available, it is usually sold on a reel and is used for wiring more delicate materials.

USEFUL EXTRAS
You will need a bucket or two to keep your flowers and foliage in, and to catch drips when hanging floral-foam based wreaths. A knife is always handy (especially for cutting floral foam). We use floral spray paint in some of the projects, it's particularly good for enhancing or changing leaf colours and can really transform a wreath. A flower frog (designed to sit at the bottom of a vase or bowl, with holes or mesh to hold flowers and foliage) is useful for arranging leftover stems and sprigs; flower frogs come in a number of designs and sizes. For some of the projects where the wreath is dressed while hanging in position, you may need a step ladder. Before you start, make sure the step ladder is set up properly and sitting on an even surface.

Types of wreaths

FROM TOP TO BOTTOM:

PLANT VINE
This is available in different thicknesses and is how we make most of our wreath bases as it also looks really wild and natural. You can use any type of plant vine, these include clematis, grape vine, wisteria and honeysuckle.

TREATED VINE WREATH
These come pre-weaved into sturdy and attractive wreath shapes, and are often made from willow. They are treated with colour and varnished.

EMBROIDERY HOOP
This gives a very basic wooden base. Anything ring-shaped like this will work for making a simple wreath.

RUSTIC WIRE
This is 18-gauge wire that has been coated in twine, such as jute, and is easy to bend into shape and wrap around to make a small, simple wreath frame.

COPPER WREATH FRAME
This makes a really handy base as there are so many points to attach things to. We also think they look very pretty as they are. This wreath frame's appearance is often enhanced when some of the copper wire is exposed or peeping through the foliage.

PLASTIC-BACKED FLORAL FOAM WREATH
These are perfect for when you want to use fresh flowers to make a lush and vibrant-looking wreath that will last for a few days.

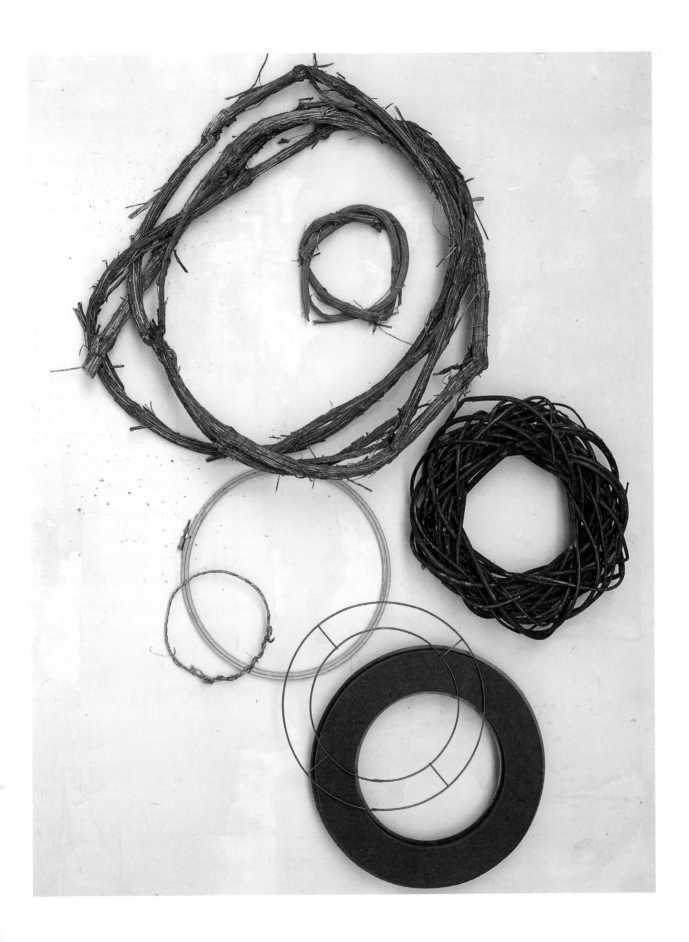

Basic wreath shape

CREATE AN ORGANIC WREATH SHAPE FROM A PLANT VINE

This is very straightforward. The vine is really malleable (we used a clematis vine here) and can be bent into a wreath shape very easily.

You may want to loop the vine around itself a few times, depending on how thick the vine is and how you would like it to look. For thick vines, just one loop with a small overlap to fix the ends together is usually sufficient; for thin, delicate vine, use three or four loops to ensure that it feels sturdy. For extra security bind together with a short piece of twine.

MATERIALS

One plant vine; the length depends
  on how big you want the wreath
  to be, and how thick the vine is
Secateurs
Twine or roll of binding wire
Bonsai scissors or florist's scissors

TIP

▷ You can keep the pieces of vine that you cut off at the start and use them to make a miniature wreath or the base of a mobile.

INSTRUCTIONS

1 Use secateurs to cut the vine to the length that you need.

2 Begin by bending the vine into the size you want the wreath to be, and then start to weave the vine around itself once or twice to give a rough circle shape (it doesn't have to be a perfect circle).

3 Using twine or binding wire, tie the vine together tightly at three or four points around the circle to make sure it is completely secure. Weave in the end to conceal it and stop it from poking out.

4 Snip off any excess twine.

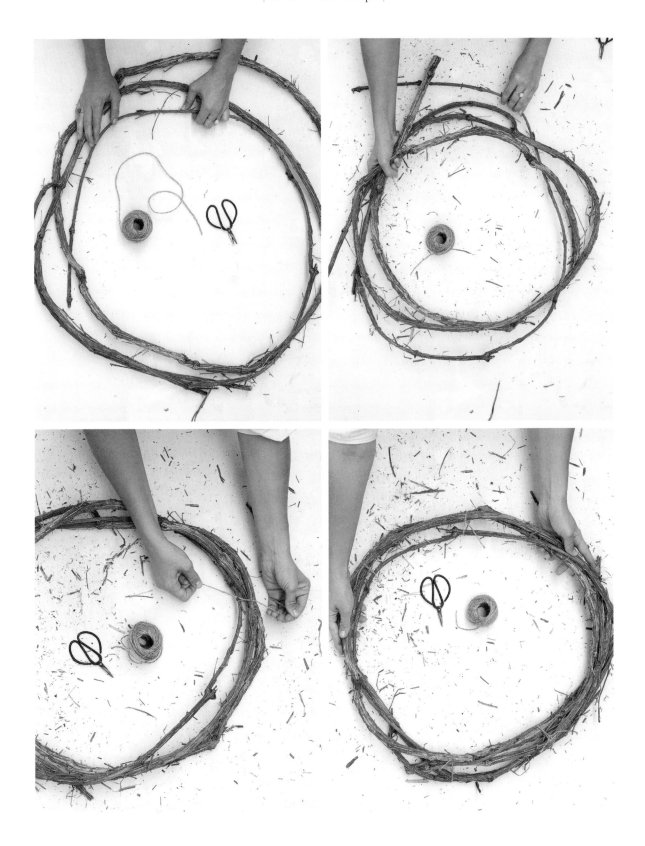

How to soak floral foam

FOR A FRESH DESIGN

Floral foam is really great for creating flow and form in a wreath, and for keeping flowers alive for longer. However, it is extremely important that the foam is soaked correctly, otherwise the centre will stay dry and the flowers will have no water to drink. Here are instructions for soaking a foam brick and a plastic-backed foam wreath.

INSTRUCTIONS FOR A FOAM BRICK

1 Fill a sink or a bucket with cold water. Make sure there is enough water to cover the brick completely once it has sunk to the bottom. You will be surprised how much water these blocks need to soak fully!

2 Float the brick gently on top of the water. Do not push it under the water or pour water on top of it. It needs to sink to the bottom by itself gradually so that the water can penetrate the entire brick.

3 Once the brick is resting at the bottom it is ready to use.

PLASTIC-BACKED FOAM WREATH

The plastic on the back of these wreaths is great as it stops the floral foam from marking the wall, or whatever it is resting on, and also makes hanging a wreath much easier. However, it does prevent the floral foam from being able to sink down into the water on its own and become fully soaked.

1 Fill a sink or bucket with cold water.

2 Float the shape with the foam side down in the water. Leave in the water for at least 15 minutes to ensure that the water has been able to soak right to the back of the foam.

TIPS

▷ If your shape is unusual and will not fit in a bucket, sink or bath, you can use a hose or a jug to pour cold water over the shape. This will take some time, so it helps if you use a needle to create small holes in the foam to encourage the water to soak through to the middle. When the foam stops soaking up water you know it is full.

▷ Keep your floral foam moist by spraying it with water from time to time. This helps to maintain your stems, keeping them fresh so you can get the most from your wreath.

Wiring

EFFECTIVE AND SECURE

Wiring is a great technique to use when you are making something that needs to be really secure. It is easy and very effective, and you can choose a wire colour that blends in nicely with your other materials.

There are lots of different types of wire you can use for different methods of wiring. Binding wire and stub wires are particularly useful when making wreaths.

INSTRUCTIONS FOR BINDING WIRE ON A ROLL

This is great for garlanding as it is on a roll and is very thin. It keeps the materials in place while you add more and is so much faster than using individual wires every time you want to attach a flower or some foliage.

INSTRUCTIONS FOR INDIVIDUAL FLORISTRY STUB WIRES

When attaching a stem to a base it is best to use individual wires. You can either cut your own from a roll of binding wire, or buy pre-cut stub wires, which are sold in a number of different lengths and thicknesses, and are widely available coated in a green lacquer.

INSTRUCTIONS

1 Simply place a flower onto the base and start to wrap the wire around the stem and the base, being careful to leave a loose end at the starting point so that you can wrap the two ends together when you have finished. Wrap around 4 or 5 times until it feels secure.

2 Then take the two ends of the wire, twist them together and push the twist down so that it is not facing outwards and is safe to touch. Snip off any excess wire using wire cutters.

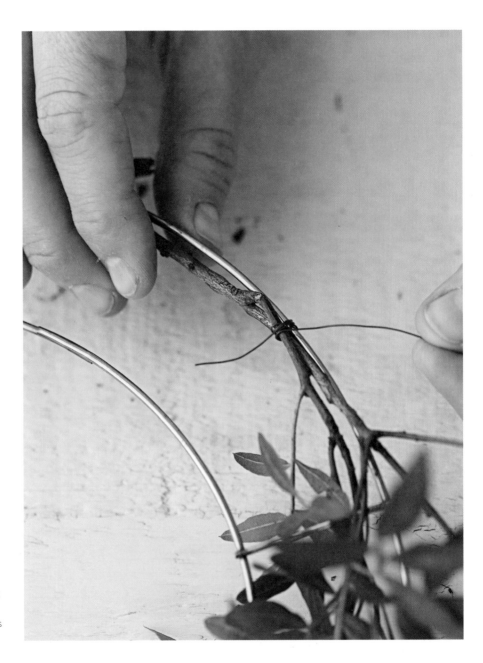

TIP

▷ To speed things up pre-cut several pieces of wire to the length required. They'll then be ready for when you start attaching the stems to your wreath.

Fresh

FIVE PROJECTS THAT CELEBRATE
FRESH SEASONAL BLOOMS

With each season, there is something new and fresh in bloom

We always try to work in tandem with the seasons, and this is one of the things that makes our job so interesting; as the seasons are always changing we constantly get to work with a new range of materials. There isn't a week that goes by in which a new flower won't have come into bloom. We feel so lucky to be connected to nature in this way and to get to view at close hand how the seasons and their flowers evolve.

There is nothing better than seeing the first daffodils of spring; lush, giant peonies in early summer; the beautiful orange leaves on beech branches in autumn or lichen-covered twigs in winter. No matter what the time of year, fresh flowers and foliage can be used to create something special.

Smelling your favourite flower can evoke so many emotions. It's lovely when a customer asks for a specific flower within an arrangement because they love the smell, or associate it with a special memory.

When making a project, each fresh flower has a purpose to fulfil. We may choose a bright pink dahlia to work as our focal flower, the one that is most eye-catching. We might use wax flowers that get to work filling in any gaps. Chocolate cosmos has such an interesting and organic shape to it that we often use it to add some flow and movement to a piece. We are also very drawn to simple wild flowers and tend to use them a lot, some of which are even regarded as weeds!

As fresh flowers used in wreaths will only last a few days, you need to take great care to get as much beauty as you can out of their short lives. To do this you need to make sure they are properly conditioned. Remove any excess leaves, then snip about 5cm (2in) from the stem on the diagonal, before placing them in water for a good drink. Take care not to knock the flower heads as this will cause them to bruise very quickly. Treat foliage in the same way, trimming 5cm (2in) from the end of the stem at a diagonal. Remove the leaves from about another 5–7cm (2–3in) to leave a short length of stem leaf-free.

There are a few interesting tricks that can help fresh flowers look their best and last as long as possible. With flowers such as roses, whose heads can be tight and take a few days to open, add a little warm water to their buckets. This encourages them to open faster, allowing you to have a flower that blooms more beautifully for your project. Adding a teaspoon of bleach to your flower buckets also helps extend the life of a cut flower by ensuring that no bacteria can form.

We try to source all our plant materials from our local flower market, using as many blooms as we can that grow in the counties around us. We think that British flowers in season are generally better quality than those that have travelled a long way to be here. However, during the winter months we do have to use imported flowers, as the options available to us are considerably reduced.

Our all-time favourite way to source flowers is to pick them ourselves. Living in the city means we don't often have the chance, but we both come from families with a parent who has a garden, so when we return home we run straight outside to pick whatever is growing. We love the fact that flowers from the garden never look perfect – they always have an oddly shaped petal or a drooping stem. This makes them so much more interesting. It goes without saying that the less perfect a flower is and the more character it has, the more we love it!

Rose chair wreath

PERFECT FOR A GATHERING

Small, simple things can often be the most meaningful.

Easy to make, this beautiful wreath adds that little something extra to a table setting. With its delicate blooms, it is the perfect accompaniment to any summer gathering. Sometimes it's hard to know how to add that floral touch – especially when limited for space – but this wreath does just that and is something your guests can take away with them at the end of the meal.

We are always looking for different and unusual ways to bring interesting little details to our events and this wreath does that perfectly. Often a popular addition to wedding sets-ups, simply add a ribbon and tie it to the back of the bride and groom's chairs to make them look really special.

Using fresh flowers does mean it will only last for a short time, you could use long-lasting or dried materials instead if you wanted it to last longer.

MATERIALS

Bonsai scissors
1 embroidery hoop
Green florist's tape
Strip of linen or ribbon (optional)

FLOWERS + FOLIAGE

4 stems of clary sage
2 stems of common yarrow stems
2 stems of cotoneaster
4 small stems of garden roses,
    (we used *Rosa* 'The Fairy')
1 stem of jasmine
2 sprigs of rosemary
1 stem of ruscus

INSTRUCTIONS

1 Prepare all your materials. Cut your flower stems diagonally, leaving approximately 8cm (just over 3in). Cut most of your foliage stems diagonally to about 16cm (6in) and leave a few of the more delicate stems slightly longer than this. Make sure you set aside one piece of foliage to add as a finishing touch – here we used a jasmine stem, about 24cm (9in) long.

2 Start by attaching the greenery to the embroidery hoop. Ruscus makes a good base foliage and also helps to give the wreath a nice flowing shape. To keep the wreath neat and tidy, attach all the materials using florist's tape. Pull the tape tight so that it becomes almost transparent, this will ensure that it will stick to itself once it is wrapped around the stem and the ring. In this wreath, the flowers are grouped together at the bottom of the wreath to provide a focal point, with foliage arranged to splay out on either side.

Add the other foliage pieces one at a time, spreading each piece out so that it covers as much of the ring as you want. Each time you add a new stem, make sure you cover the tape from the previous joining. If you add all the materials in the same direction this is easy to achieve.

3 Once all the greenery has been added, you can begin to attach the flowers. Use tape around the stems to secure the flowers to the ring; always try to cover the tape from the previous flower when you add each new one. Add your flowers in any order you like, but for visual impact it is a good idea to add the larger blooms in groups. Here the garden roses are close together, which strengthens the overall visual balance of the wreath. These larger-headed flowers also help to cover any areas of tape that are still visible.

4 When you have added all your flowers, finish by inserting a final piece of foliage under the head of one of the larger flowers, going in the opposite direction to the rest of the wreath. Something delicate, such as jasmine, works very well. Rather than taping this in place, it is usually possible just to wrap the stem around the ring, or place it in gently through a gap between the flowers and the foliage.

Then either loop the hoop onto the side of a chair or tie some linen or a ribbon to the top and attach it to the back of a chair with a bow.

TIPS

▷ If you would like this wreath to last for longer than one event, choose flowers with woody stems such as protea, common yarrow 'Parker's Variety', or heather or alternatively choose blooms that will dry out well.

▷ Any base can be used for this project, it doesn't have to be an embroidery hoop – you can make the same wreath using wire or vine.

Descending rope wreath

CREATE THE UNEXPECTED

Being asked to make a large, impactful display can be a daunting prospect, and if we are being honest, we are always looking for ways to simplify things. It is much less complicated to make one large display out of a number of smaller parts. This is because you can make them one by one in a relatively small space, and they are generally easy to transport, put up and take back down again.

Playing around with different heights within a space is visually more interesting than keeping everything at the same level. This works particularly well in spaces with high ceilings and beams as it naturally provides something to hang multiple wreaths from and create an impressive display, perfect for a dinner

party. If you don't have a large space in which to hang this installation, then you can scale it down to fit your space. That's what is great about this project, you could make a tiny version for a small gathering in your kitchen, or a much larger version for a wedding or a big occasion.

These wreaths were made using fresh flowers and foliage, so only really last for the duration of the event, but you could do the same design using dried or longer-lasting materials. If you didn't fancy using a decking rope, then try a coloured rope or strong string that will complement your wreaths, especially if you are making a smaller-scaled version of this design. Get as creative as you like with these wreaths.

MATERIALS

3 different lengths of clematis vine,
   each one between 2.5 and 4m
   (8–13ft) in length
Florist's scissors
Twine
Step ladder (optional)
Manila natural rope, 6m (about
   20ft) in length

FLOWERS + FOLIAGE

3 stems of blackberry bush
   with foliage
6 stems of chocolate cosmos
1 common ivy vine, roughly
   50cm (20in) in length
2 stems of coneflower
1 orange dahlia
8 stems of eucalyptus
6 stems of helenium
3 stems of jasmine foliage
4 stems of pistachio foliage
5 poppy pods
1 stem of ruscus foliage
5 stems of white scabiosa
2 stems of smoke bush foliage
3 wild grasses

INSTRUCTIONS

1 Make three basic vine wreath bases in different sizes (see page 18). Lay the wreath bases on the ground in the approximate layout you intend to hang them. The length of the stems of the flowers and foliage you use is up to you. If you want a wild looking display, keep the stems longer, allowing them to flow outwards from your wreaths. If you prefer a tidier looking display, cut the stems shorter and tie them close to the wreath bases.

2 Using twine, start by tying the foliage stems to each wreath base. Cover the string with the foliage and stems you are adding as you go. The aim is to add enough foliage to each one, while at the same time leaving some of the beautiful vine base on show. Consider the flow of your designs. For one wreath, for example, you might arrange one side to be heavier with flowers and foliage than the other, a pleasing combination. For this, fix several stems facing in one direction and counterbalance these with just a few stems arranged to mirror the fuller side.

3 When you are happy with the arrangement of foliage, next add the flowers with the sturdiest stems. Attach them where you think they look best – for example, group some to form a focal point, and sprinkle the rest throughout the wreath – making sure that each wreath includes a few flowers. It is best to keep the more delicate flowers to one side while the wreaths start to take shape and add them at the end when the wreaths are hung.

4 Once you are happy with the overall coverage on each wreath it is time to hang them on the rope. Suspend the rope from an existing beam or from hooks screwed into the ceiling and secure with a knot – you may need to use a step ladder here in order to reach. This display works well when the wreaths hang at different heights. Loop your first wreath through the rope and decide on the height at which it looks best. Once you are happy with this, attach the rope to the top of the fixture and hang your next wreath to a section of the rope. Continue to do this until all your wreaths are hung and then tie up the remaining rope, securing everything tightly.

5 Finally, add your delicate flowers to the wreaths. You should not need to tie many of these, as it should be possible to simply feed them into the existing string. If you do need to tie them, do so loosely and gently so they do not become damaged.

TIPS

▷ As well as deciding on the heights of your wreath, you will also want to consider the spacing between them. In larger areas the wreaths can be spread out, while in smaller spaces they will need to be grouped closely together.

▷ We love it when some of the wreath vine is visible through the foliage, but if you prefer your wreaths to be covered the whole way around you will probably need to double the number of stems used.

▷ You can keep the basic wreath shapes to use again, just strip off all the flowers and foliage once they have been used.

▷ If you have any leftover stems, you can use them to make little table arrangements to complement the main hanging display. This will help to tie the table decorations and the backdrop together.

Meadow ball

VERSATILE AND DRAMATIC

We are often asked to make something unexpected and unusual, a decorative piece that will surprise people, and this cloud-like meadow ball does just that!

It is easy to shy away from making large hanging pieces for your home because they may be too big and complicated. Don't be afraid to be creative and scale this project up or down depending on what your space will allow.

This project is as dramatic as it looks, but is also incredibly simple to make. It is extremely versatile too and can be made for all sorts of occasions – simply swap in different blooms to create a different effect depending on what you are making it for. We have created giant, peony-filled balls for weddings, and smaller, delicate, wildflower versions for birthday suppers. It can be the main centrepiece, hanging indoors above a dining table, but will look just as beautiful suspended from the branch of a tree over a summer picnic.

As floral foam is used for the base of this design, the flowers you use will last for a few days. Make sure you spray your foam regularly to keep your flowers fresh.

MATERIALS

2 metal circular hanging baskets,
   30cm (12in) in diameter
3 blocks of floral foam
Florist's scissors
Knife
8 cable ties
Natural cotton rope or linen,
   4m (13ft) in length
Bucket
Step ladder (optional)
Screw hook for hanging, if required

FLOWERS + FOLIAGE

6 stems of white achillea
10 stems of cow parsley
15 stems of japanese anemone
6 stems of flowering mint
6 stems of pistachio foliage
4 poppy pods
15 stems of smoke bush

TIPS

▷ Hanging baskets come in all
different sizes, so you can make
your ball as big or small as you like.

▷ You can make a feature of
how the ball is hung by choosing
different types of rope or chain.

INSTRUCTIONS

1 Start by removing the chain section of your hanging baskets. Soak three blocks of floral foam (see page 20). While the floral foam is soaking, cut the stems diagonally to length. For this project, the stems are 30cm (12in), or even longer, so that the finished ball looks large and wild.

2 Place one and a half pieces of soaked floral foam into each basket. The foam is easy to cut with a knife dry or wet and the amount you use will depend on the size of your baskets. Place one basket on top of the other to create a sphere, with the floral foam inside, and then seal them together as tightly as you can, using cable ties all the way around. It does not matter if the foam is bulging out in places – you don't need the sides to be smooth unless you want to create a very neat and tidy ball. If you are, then use the knife to cut away the excess foam until you have the circular shape you want.

3 Once you have sealed your ball, take your rope and tie it on tightly with a double knot; a point somewhere along the seal works best to ensure everything stays together. It is easier to hang the ball in place before placing any stems into it, so use the rope to suspend the ball in position. Place a bucket under the ball as water from the foam will drip for a while when you start to add your stems. You can now start placing your flowers and foliage into the ball – you may need to stand on a step ladder in order to work on your design. When using a mix of flowers and foliage, it is best to add the foliage first, aiming to cover as much of the floral foam and basket structure as you can. For this project, add the smoke bush first, as it is the main foliage.

4 Once you have a basic covering of foliage over the ball, and the frame is no longer visible, you can start to add the flowers. Use the flowers with the sturdiest looking stems first and dot them around the ball, ensuring there is an even number of flowers on each side. Finally, place the more delicate flowers where they will catch the eye. Keep adding flowers until the ball is as wild as you want it to look; the aim is for this piece to look lush and unstructured as if it is growing in mid-air.

Wild spring wreath

A LITTLE PATCH OF WILD GARDEN INDOORS

Without a doubt spring is one of the most wonderful times of year. It is hard to beat that feeling you get when the flowers and trees start to bloom, and you know that there are many months ahead of being able to use all your favourite flowers. As florists, we always have to get up early, and the cold, dark winter mornings make this particularly hard. But when the season starts to change, the weather gets warmer and the days brighten it makes being up with the dawn a much nicer and easier experience.

We love the concept of a seasonal wreath: the idea that you can celebrate any season and the fact that this brings you a little closer to nature and the ever-changing world around you. You can go for a walk, take a few cuttings and make a wreath that really reflects and celebrates what is growing around you.

This is a really simple project and the base can be used again and again. As the fresh flowers won't be kept in water, it is best used for a gathering or special occasion. The upside of this is that you can make it look different every time. The willow pre-made wreath base is treated with varnish and looks attractive in its own right, so there is no need to cover the whole shape if you prefer not to.

This wreath will brighten up any space, bringing a little patch of wild garden inside. It also works well hanging in the hallway, giving the feeling that you have brought a piece of springtime with you into your home.

MATERIALS

Florist's scissors
1 pre-made natural willow plaited
    vine wreath
Linen or rope to hang
Nail or hook for hanging, if required

FLOWERS + FOLIAGE

7 stems of white achillea
10 stems of yellow achillea
8 stems of purple flowering basil
3 stems of purple clematis
8 stems of cotoneaster foliage
2 stems of white delphinium
5 stems of fennel
5 stems of lavender leaf foliage
5 stems of flowering mint
7 stems of wax flower
10 wild grasses

TIPS

▷ Choose flowers with woody
stems, such as wax flowers and
hydrangeas, which will last longer
out of water. Flowers with hollow
stems, such as daffodils or poppies,
can die quickly, so be mindful of
this when you are choosing your
flowers.

▷ This is a good project to make
with flowers that will dry out well,
such as achillea 'Parker's Variety',
wild heather or woody stemmed
hydrangeas.

INSTRUCTIONS

1 Prepare your chosen stems by cutting them diagonally into a
variety of different lengths, approximately 30cm (12in) for the
longer, wilder stems and 15cm (6in) for the stems that will sit
tighter to the wreath's base. Start at the top and weave your
foliage stems in a clockwise direction through the plait of the
vine. There is no need to wire or tape the foliage in place as the
wreath structure is tight enough to hold the stems securely. This
type of wreath looks best when the flowers and foliage are placed
following the same direction; this helps give the wreath a good
shape and flow.

2 Continue to cover the base of your wreath with foliage until
you feel that you have a good basic coverage. Place them in
a diagonal direction as opposed to straight in, following the
direction of the base. Then add your flowers, once again in
a clockwise direction, where you feel they are needed and
where they look best, making sure each area has some floral
embellishment. It is just as effective to add your flowers in
groups, or create patterns with them.

3 To hang, thread a strip of linen or rope through the back of
the structure and hang on a nail or hook screwed into the wall,
or suspended from a handy structure (we've used the bar of a
ceiling clothes dryer here).

4 The beauty of this wreath is that you literally just place your
materials into the wreath base, with no tying or taping in position.
This means that it is quick to make and can be easily changed if
there is anything you are not happy with.

Midsummer wreath

PERFECT FOR A GATHERING

Summer is most florists' favourite time of year. We can't walk anywhere without staring into gardens bursting with flowers and wanting to pick them all!

What better way to celebrate midsummer and welcome the coming of the summer months than with a fresh floral wreath. This is one of the best times of year for flowers – this is peak season and there's a wonderful selection to choose from.

This wreath epitomises summertime and is one that you will want to show off. It would look striking hanging on a front door, but it would also be just as impressive hanging above a mantelpiece. For a midsummer party, you could lay your wreath flat on the table, perhaps even with a candle in it to create a seasonal centrepiece.

This is a great project if you have a garden that you can take a real mix of cuttings from to personalise your design. As the base for this wreath is made out of floral foam, fresh flowers will last for quite a while. Just remember to keep the floral foam wet by spraying it regularly with a water sprayer.

MATERIALS

1 plastic-backed floral foam base
    in a ring shape, 36cm (14½in)
    in diameter
2–3 buckets
Florist's scissors
Nail or hook for hanging, if required

FLOWERS + FOLIAGE

5 stems of white achillea
2 stems of wild allium
2 stems of pink anthurium
1 stem of artichoke
3 stems of coneflower
4 stems white cosmos
2 stems pink cosmos
3 stems of yellow cosmos
6 stems of cotoneaster foliage
4 stems geranium foliage
2 stems of lisianthus
7 poppy pods
2 stems of red-hot poker
3 stems of scabiosa
3 stems of strawflower
2 stems of wax flower
10 wild grasses (various)

INSTRUCTIONS

1 First, soak your floral foam (see page 20). In this project, the flowers are arranged by colour families, so begin by sorting your flowers while they are in their buckets into pinks and reds, oranges and yellow, whites, and a separate group for foliage and grasses.

2 Select the largest or most eye-catching bloom – the focal flower – from each colour group and trim the stems diagonally to about 15cm (6in). Start each colour section on the wreath by inserting a focal flower into the foam – one for pinks and reds on one side and a large bloom for yellows and oranges on the other. Place a large white flower in between to break up the hot colours. Set aside some of the longer-stemmed flowers and foliage to use later.

3 Cut the remaining flower stems diagonally to about 8cm (just over 3in), with around 4cm (1½in) of that inserted into the floral foam. It is best to cut a small selection of stems just before you place them into the foam so that there are not too many stems out of water for too long. Build up the wreath by placing the smaller flowers into their respective colour groups. Use foliage with different textures around them, and vary the stem lengths, using the photograph as a guideline. If you are using mostly foliage, cover the base first and place the flowers in at the end, so they hold most of the attention.

4 Continue to work your way around the wreath, building the colour in each section until the colour theming becomes more apparent. Make sure you continue to use a mix of foliage and flowers to cover the base and keep your wreath balanced.

5 Once the base is covered and you can't see any of the floral foam, you can start to make the wreath look a little more wild. Insert longer-stemmed flowers and foliage of varying lengths into the top and sides of the wreath to create this effect. After the floral foam is soaked it does become heavy, so if you are planning to hang it be sure that the fixings are sturdy. You can balance the wreath on a nail or wrap some wire around it before you start inserting the flowers.

TIPS

▷ The floral foam ring used here is 36cm (14½in) in diameter, but foam rings are available in a number of different sizes, so don't feel limited to using the same size as us.

▷ This piece used around 40 flower stems and 20 pieces of foliage, but there are no rules dictating what flowers to use or how many, this is just a guide. However, to keep it interesting, we recommend including a range of different shapes, textures and lengths.

▷ Use a water sprayer every few days to keep your flowers fresh. Gently stick the nozzle between the flowers to mist the foam.

▷ If you are hanging this wreath, the excess water will start to drain out of the ring, so suspend it over a basin for a few minutes before placing it on a wall or door to prevent a puddle!

▷ This is one of those projects that you can keep on adding to, so stand back and have a look every so often to make sure the wreath is not losing its shape.

Foraged

FOUR PROJECTS THAT
CELEBRATE THE SEASONS

A small creation can remind you of a special adventure

We find foraging so exciting: heading out in the morning with no idea what we will find and what it will inspire us to make.

Each season provides something completely different: winter gifts bare branches that are perfect for making mobiles, spring has beautiful sprays of blossom that can brighten any day and billows of cow parsley that fit any vase, summer is for bright and vibrant wild flowers, while autumn charms us with chestnuts, acorns and pinecones littered on pathways.

Different counties and even different authorities within them have varying rules on foraging, so be sure to check what you can gather before you head out with a basket and scissors and break the law in an ethereal manner! In the UK, it is illegal to pick from public parks and planned planting areas, such as roundabouts and public planters. And of course, we would encourage you always to be mindful and forage sustainably without harming woods or wildlife, and never uproot a whole plant so that it can't flower again in the same place. Certain plants, such as orchids and bluebells, are protected in the UK so it is best to pick flowers that are in abundance and on land where it is legal. Pick them randomly so you don't leave bare patches. Only take what you need – and be sure to leave some for the bees!

Before you go foraging, it is very important that you make yourself aware of any harmful plants that could be growing in your area. Plants such as giant hogweed may look innocent and pretty, but can be very harmful to your health if picked. Be sure to wear gloves for handling spiky stems.

Flowers are best cut in the morning or the late afternoon when they are full of nutrients and water and not stressed from the hot sun. Flowers in full bloom might not last very long, but if you pick tight buds there is a chance they will not open once cut, so it is best to snip flowers that have a slightly bigger and looser bud and are on the verge of opening. We use scissors that give a clean cut and produce a longer vase life (this can also encourage regrowth of the plant). Take secateurs if foraging for slightly woodier stems.

We pack little flower vials for water when we go foraging and pop the stems into them to make sure they don't die if the weather is hot on the way home. When you get back be sure to snip the stems diagonally and give them a good drink of water so that they will last longer.

Open your mind to what will look good in an arrangement. It is not always about the perfect-looking bloom; wild grasses and unusual shapes shake up an arrangement and set it apart from the norm. We love finding an overgrown field of grasses, and they also dry out beautifully, so you can reap the benefit all year around. Foraged stems are not to everyone's taste, however. Once we were putting boxes of wedding flowers into a cab and the driver asked us why we were filling his car with weeds!

It is incredible what a morning spent in nature can do not only for your sense of wellbeing but also for your appreciation of the natural world. Find yourself a wildflower identification book, take it with you when you go out and expand your botanical knowledge too.

Geometric foliage shapes

A SIMPLE WAY TO CREATE AN IMPACT

While wreaths are traditionally circular, we have always really enjoyed experimenting by making them using a variety of different geometric shapes.

Our friend Dale, who has a shop above our studio, brought us a simple metal triangle one day and we instantly fell in love and saw the wreath potential. He kindly made us some bespoke frames for this project. They are made from thin metal rods purchased at a model making shop, cut into pieces and soldered together to secure the shape. It is a simple process if you have access to the equipment, but if you do not want to start soldering you can also make a frame by tying twigs or branches together to form any geometric shape you want.

This pared-down display works best as a group; the shapes play off each other beautifully and the simpler your design, the better! Once you have made and hung the basic frames, you can experiment with the flowers to achieve the look you want. The frames also look great when unadorned, which is handy when life gets in the way of time for arranging flowers!

MATERIALS

3 geometric frames: a triangle 50
     x 50 x 50cm (20 x 20 x 20in), a
     rectangle 60 x 30cm (24 x 12in)
     and a 50cm (20in) square
2–3 picture nails, or picture
     rail hooks
Florist's scissors
3m (6ft) of twine, plus extra if
     hanging from picture rail hooks
2 small ceramic bowls (optional)
2 florist's flower frogs (optional)

FLOWERS + FOLIAGE

4 stems of dried grasses
12 stems of white cosmos
30 stems of cotoneaster foliage
     stripped from a branch, lengths
     varying between 10 and 30cm
     (4 and 12in)

TIPS

▷ The wonderful thing about this
project is its simplicity: it uses
only three different types of plant
material. This allows the beauty of
the shapes to shine through.

▷ If you add too heavy items to
your frames it can be difficult to get
them to sit straight on the wall; it is
best to keep things light and simple.

▷ As usual, if you want this project
to last longer then use flowers that
tend to dry well.

INSTRUCTIONS

1 First decide where each frame should be placed in the space;
in the photograph on page 59, two frames are hanging from the
wall and one is leaning against it. Secure the frames in position
using simple picture hanging tacks or suspend from a picture rail
if the room has one.

2 Next add the cotoneaster to the frames, starting with the
shorter lengths and building up to the longer pieces. Tie the
stems on with twine at two or more different points on each
shape. Cotoneaster is perfect for this project as it naturally
creates interesting shapes that feel wild and organic. Don't add
too many of the cotoneaster stems as it is nice to be able to see
the structure of the frame underneath.

3 Add the white cosmos, once again tying each flower onto the
frame using twine. Cosmos creates delicate, beautiful shapes and
work well as the feature flower in this design. Use them where
you think the frame needs more character; each frame should
have at least one. Group them with one or more stems of grass
for contrast.

4 If there is any greenery left over at the end you can use small
bowls and florist's flower frogs to create simple arrangements to
sit in front of the frames, adding to the overall display.

MATERIALS

Enough twigs or branches of
equal length to construct your
geometric shapes (see page 60
for dimensions)
11 single stub wires
Wire cutters

(see page 60 for dimensions)

TIP

▷ To make this project even wilder,
choose branches that have smaller
offshoots growing from them.

INSTRUCTIONS FOR CREATING A BRANCH FRAME

1 Select the number of twigs or branches required to create your
shapes. These can be foraged on a walk or from your garden. It is
always better to collect fallen twigs so you don't damage a living
plant or tree. Also, branches that have already fallen tend to be
drier, so are perfect to work with. Consider when choosing your
sticks if they have any peeling bark and whether you would be
happy for that to be incorporated into your final design.

2 Starting with your first shape, decide which sticks you want to
attach, taking into account that they will need to overlap slightly.
Once you have come to a decision, hold in place and start to
wrap the wire around the both twigs about 1.5cm (½in) from
the ends.

3 Keep wrapping until almost all the wire is used and the twigs
feel secure. Then take the two ends of the wire, twist them
together and push the ends down so that they are not facing
outwards and the wire is safe to touch. If there is a lot of leftover
wire, use cutters to snip off the excess.

4 Continue this for all the corners until your shape is secure.
Follow the same procedure for the other two shapes.

Mirror garland

A SCENTED KITCHEN DECORATION

This project uses basic garlanding, and once you've mastered it on a small scale, you'll be able to adorn your staircase banisters and mantelpieces with wonderful garlands.

In Ireland where we grew up, it is common to decorate mirrors and frames with local holly or ivy at Christmas time and shamrocks on St. Patrick's Day, but the garland in this project is lovely for

any time of year, whether you are having a celebration, or just want to fill your home with delicious scents.

This seasonal project is perfect for decorating a mirror in a small kitchen or adorning a hallway, especially when you make it with scented herbs and luscious greenery, which continue to look and smell good even when they have dried out.

MATERIALS

Florist's scissors
1 circular mirror, approximately
    60cm (24in) in diameter
Wire cutters
Rustic wire, 5cm (2in) longer than
    the diameter of the mirror
Roll of binding wire

FLOWERS + FOLIAGE

5 stems of lavender foliage
5 stems of mimosa foliage
10 stems of pistachio foliage
5 stems of rosemary foliage
5 stems of sage

TIPS

▷ You can make a garland on a larger
scale using more exotic foliage,
such as palm leaves.

▷ When you are wiring, to start with
the tips of your fingers may start
to hurt from pulling the wire tight
– this is an occupational hazard of
being a florist. You could always
wear a pair of gardening gloves or
have some nice hand cream ready
to soothe and soften your fingers
afterwards.

INSTRUCTIONS

1 Cut each piece of foliage to approximately 20cm (8in),
including the stem. Measure the frame around which you are
working and using wire cutters, cut a piece of rustic wire to the
same size, adding about 5cm (2in) to allow for tying the ends.

2 Place one small piece of foliage about 3cm (just over 1in)
along the rustic wire. Bind the stem of the foliage to the rustic
wire using binding wire, wrapping it tightly a few times so that it
is secure.

3 Then take two or three stems together in a little bundle, place
them on top of the stem you have just wired, and bind over that
stem; you only need to bind each bundle 1–2 times, pulling the
wire tightly each time.

4 Continue to do this, mixing various herbs and foliage to add
different textures and tones of green, gradually building up the
bundles if you want to create a thicker garland, to a given point.
The aim is to frame just under half the diameter of the mirror.

5 As you reach the section at which you want the garland to
finish, start to make the bundles smaller so that the end point of
the garland appears to taper off naturally and the last wire will not
be noticeable.

6 Once you have added the last bundle, snip the binding wire and
secure it tightly around the last piece of foliage. Wrap the garland
around the mirror or your frame, and where the two ends meet
twist them tightly together so that they stay on the frame. Use
the wire cutters to snip any excess wire that you don't need.

Late summer chandelier

FORAGE THE FINAL FLOWERS OF SUMMER

This wreath was made for a late summer dinner we held for a few of our friends. It is the time of year when everyone has returned from their holidays, the night air is beginning to cool and we all gravitate indoors wanting to be warm and cosy. Foraging around this time of year is wonderful: the final flowers of the summer, such as Japanese anemones, are in bloom and there are the first creeping signs of autumn, with crab apples and rosehips starting to appear.

For this wreath, we stumbled upon a mountain of rosehips along the canal path, and we knew when we saw them that they would be perfect for our creation. We wanted it to feel foraged and that is why the rosehip branches work so well — they naturally give you wild and beautiful shapes.

A wreath chandelier is an impressive addition to most spaces. We always like the idea of surprising our guests with a hanging piece as it's less obvious and creates a festive atmosphere. It is also nice to keep the table clear (to allow for more food and wine) and this wreath does just that.

MATERIALS

1 basic vine wreath base, 2m
(7ft) in diameter
Twine
3 x 1m (3ft) lengths of window sash
cord (or other strong rope),
7mm thick, to hang
Step ladder (optional)
Secateurs
A screw hook if you don't have
ceiling beams

FLOWERS + FOLIAGE

4 long stems of rosehips with lots
of foliage and berries

TIPS

▷ If you have room on your table,
you can always add a few sprigs
of rosehips, which will help marry
the table and your hanging
display together.

▷ Lots of foraged materials we
use tend to be spiky, when this is
the case use gardening gloves to
protect your hands.

INSTRUCTIONS

1 Make a basic vine wreath (see page 18). The next thing to do is hang it – it is much easier to do this before adding any of the rosehip stems. Tie the three lengths of sash cord to three points around the wreath base using a secure knot, making sure that there is equal space between each length of rope. If you don't have a beam or an existing fixing from which to suspend your wreath, you can use a hook screwed into the ceiling. Use a step ladder to hang the wreath, making sure the ladder is set up properly and on an even surface before standing on it. This is also a great wreath for an outdoor gathering – suspend your wreath from a branch over a tree so it can hang daintily above your table or picnic rug.

2 Once the wreath base is hung and balanced, you can start to drape the rosehip stems. Use twine to secure the rosehips at various points around the wreath. Keep the wreath looking loose and natural, allowing some longer pieces to hang down.

3 Stand back to view the wreath from all angles while you work. When you feel you have added enough, check that it is still level; if the wreath has become unbalanced, you may need to adjust the ropes securing it to the ceiling, or add more foliage to the lighter side until it balances itself out.

Copper foliage wreath

BRING SOME WILD ELEGANCE INDOORS

This wreath is elegant and inexpensive to make. It can be adapted for all seasons and can be a permanent decorative piece in your home using whatever is fresh and long-lasting.

Foliage such as pistachio, ruscus and mimosa are ideal for a project like this as they keep their shape out of water. Flowers or foliage with woody stems that have their own structure are good choices – wild and not too straight and uniform. We also felt that the copper frame was so attractive that we didn't want to cover it all, and so left a small section on show.

Copper frames are available in all different sizes, so the world is your oyster. A huge one decorated with a variety of fresh, romantic foliage would make a lovely backdrop to a summer wedding, but a small one would look just as good in your bedroom.

MATERIALS

Wire cutters
Roll of binding wire (or any other
    floristry wire)
Florist's scissors
1 copper wreath frame, 30cm
    (12in) in diameter
Hook or nail for hanging, if required
Ribbon, 50cm (20in) in length
Twine (optional)

FLOWERS + FOLIAGE

1 stem of fresh clematis foliage
2 stems of jasmine
6 stems of pistachio foliage
2 stems of variegated pittosporum

TIPS

▷ To give this wreath a seasonal
flavour you could wire in blossom
in spring, small cuttings of fruiting
branches such as blackberry or
raspberry in summer, acorns or
chestnuts in autumn, or pine cones
in winter.

▷ This wreath looks nice when it
is left loose and natural although
classically these frames were
designed to be stuffed with moss
for a bulkier living wreath.

INSTRUCTIONS

1 Start by getting your materials ready. Use the wire cutters to
cut about ten 3cm (1½in) pieces of binding or other floristry wire.
The thinner the wire, the less foliage you will need to cover it up.
Set aside a few longer stems for later. Cut the rest of the stems
to approximately 18cm (7in), including any actual stem. Put the
smaller pieces to one side to use as fillers in Step 3.

2 Working in a clockwise direction, begin to add shape to your
wreath. Weave the woody stems of the foliage around the frame
and then use a piece of wire to secure it onto the outer frame
of the ring, wrapping the wire around until everything is secure.
Place another piece of foliage just on top of where you wrapped
the wire and secure that piece further down the frame.

3 Continue to add foliage to cover the wiring, but be sure to
choose pieces of foliage with a good shape, or that will bend
easily and follow the shape of the frame. You can also wire a
few smaller pieces to the inside ring of the frame, but keep
these small so that they do not fill the hole in the centre and
cause the shape of the wreath to be lost.

4 When you get to the bottom of the frame, start to add
foliage to the top of the other side, working your way round
in an anticlockwise direction. For this wreath, we grouped the
clematis leaves close to the top of the wreath to a give a bold,
asymmetrical focal point. Where the two points meet, there
will be a mesh of woody stems that make it easier to feed in the
bottom foliage. However, continue to secure each piece with
small wires to ensure that nothing falls out when you hang the
wreath. Finally add a few long, wild stems to give the desired flow.

5 Feed one piece of ribbon through the outer ring at the bottom
of the frame and let it hang down. To fix the wreath to the wall,
you can hang the frame directly from a hook or nail, or you
can attach a ribbon or twine to the top and use this to hang
the frame.

Dried

SIX PROJECTS THAT
ARE PERFECT TO KEEP

A flower that lasts two springs

It is very rewarding when a flower you love dries out beautifully. It provides another chance to be creative, and allows you to arrange your flowers in new and different ways. The transformation from fresh to dried varies, at times the change is subtle, but it is often quite pronounced. Sometimes a rather boring fresh flower really comes into its own when it has dried. Everything deserves a second chance!

So much of floristry is based around fresh flowers, but as we all know, they only last a few days. It is wonderful to be able to create something that will last for a long time, especially when making a gift or something for the home.

There is not nearly the same choice of flowers during the winter months. Our solution is to stockpile summer flowers we have dried so that there are more options to work with out of season.

Another benefit of dried flowers and foliage is that they take spray paint and paint really well. Sometimes when we want to add a touch of colour to a project, we will spray a few of our dried materials. The advantage is that you can use any colour you like, and your project will look that little bit more unique.

Some of our favourite plants to dry out are big tropical leaves, such as fan palms. We always have a selection of these drying out in our studio. The shapes, colours and textures of these leaves when dried is wonderful; they are visually striking and work extremely well within the home.

There are many ways to dry flowers: air drying, pressing and sand drying are some of processes we use a lot. Air drying is the easiest technique to dry flowers. This can be as simple as hanging them upside down in bundles, but always make sure that the environment isn't damp, as this will encourage bacteria to grow between the stems and the bundle will start to rot. Remember to strip flowers of any foliage before hanging them. A dark, well-ventilated room is the best place to air dry. Chicken wire grids are good for flowers with big heads. Simply place the stem through the holes with the flower heads balanced on top.

Little flower heads and small sprigs of foliage are ideal for pressing, and any leftovers provide a steady supply for the flower press. These look simple and pretty on invitations, dinner menus or greeting cards, and we are frequently asked for them.

Dried flowers work well when mixed with fresh flowers too. They can add a harder, spiky texture to any creation, giving it that something extra. Dried grasses are also good to use as they can provide a softer, more fluffy texture to work with.

Some of the flowers that we think look great when dried include mimosa, hydrangea, achillea 'Parker's Variety', allium (ornamental onion), nigella (love-in-a-mist) pods, scabious, quaking grass, safflower, pampas grass, globe thistles, strawflower, sea lavender, fan palm and poppy pods.

Flower wall

THE SIMPLEST OF IDEAS CAN TURN OUT TO BE THE MOST EFFECTIVE

Sometimes the simplest of ideas can turn out to be the most effective, and things don't get much simpler than a flower wall. All you need is some tape and flower snippings – and a wall of course!

You can create a small flower wall over your bed using lavender and rosemary, which may aid peaceful sleep (we heard also an old wives' tale that roses in the bedroom prevent nightmares), but we can't promise anything!

It's a project that can be made with a group of friends: Terri made one of these walls for a friend's wedding. It was the perfect way to get everybody involved. In the end, all the wedding photographs were taken against it; the wall made the perfect backdrop and it was something that many of the guests felt proud to have had a hand in creating.

Neither of us are very good at making anything very linear, it's just not in our nature, and when it comes to measuring things precisely we just don't find it much fun. Therefore, we always lean on the side of irregular shapes. However, this project does work well when made symmetrically, if you have the time and patience to measure everything out exactly!

This wall is made up of dried materials, so after the dinner party or gathering is over there is no rush to take it down.

MATERIALS

2 rolls of masking tape, plus
    extra if marking out a design
Bonsai scissors

FLOWERS + FOLIAGE

10 stems of dried achillea
10 stems of preserved fern
40 dried mixed grasses
10 stems of small dried honesty
10 stems of dried lady's mantle
10 stems of dried lavender
10 dried nigella seed pods
3 stems of dried Northern sea oats
20 dried poppy pods
10 stems of preserved ruscus
10 stems of dried sea-lavender
10 stems of dried wheat

This wall uses approximately 160 dried stems. As very small pieces are used, in most cases you can get many individual sprigs out of a single stem.

TIPS

▷ You can experiment with many different types of tape when making this wall. We favour plain masking tape, but you could use washi tape if you want to add more colour.

▷ You can also produce other effects using masking tape when preparing the area to be covered — for example, use it to create stripes down a wall and fill in every second stripe with taped flowers. When you remove the masking tape you will be left with stripes of flowers on the wall.

INSTRUCTIONS

1 Plan how much of the wall you want to fill and what overall shape you want to make. This project uses an abstract unsymmetrical shape, but if you want to create a geometric design, such as a perfect square, it is a good idea to mark this out on the wall using masking tape before you start.

2 Cut all your stems in preparation for them to be taped onto the wall. For this project, use small pieces measuring approximately 15cm (6in). Prepare some tape strips approximately 7cm (3in) in length to speed up the process.

3 Next, start sticking your stems to the wall, beginning in the middle and working your way out. Treat the process as a jigsaw, always making sure that each piece fits well with its neighbour. You can also turn stems upside down and place them on the diagonal to ensure everything feels balanced. This makes it easier to achieve a good flow.

4 Take a step back every so often and have a look at what you have created. Make sure you avoid putting two of the same stems next to each other and fill in any visible gaps.

5 There is no real end point for this project; just stop when you feel happy with how it looks.

Rustic wall hanging

USE LITTLE FORAGED THINGS YOU FOUND ON A WALK

This is another wonderfully easy project and is a lovely way of remembering a special place or day by picking some stems and other little foraged things to hang daintily in your home.

The wall hanging looks great with foliage or dried flowers, but daintier materials always seem to work better. This is great for decorating a bedroom or a hallway wall and can be changed seasonally by adding stems of different dried flowers. The best thing about this project is that there are no rules; you can add whatever you find and have dried. Keep it simple and elegant, or add feathers, conkers and pine cones you have found on a walk in the countryside.

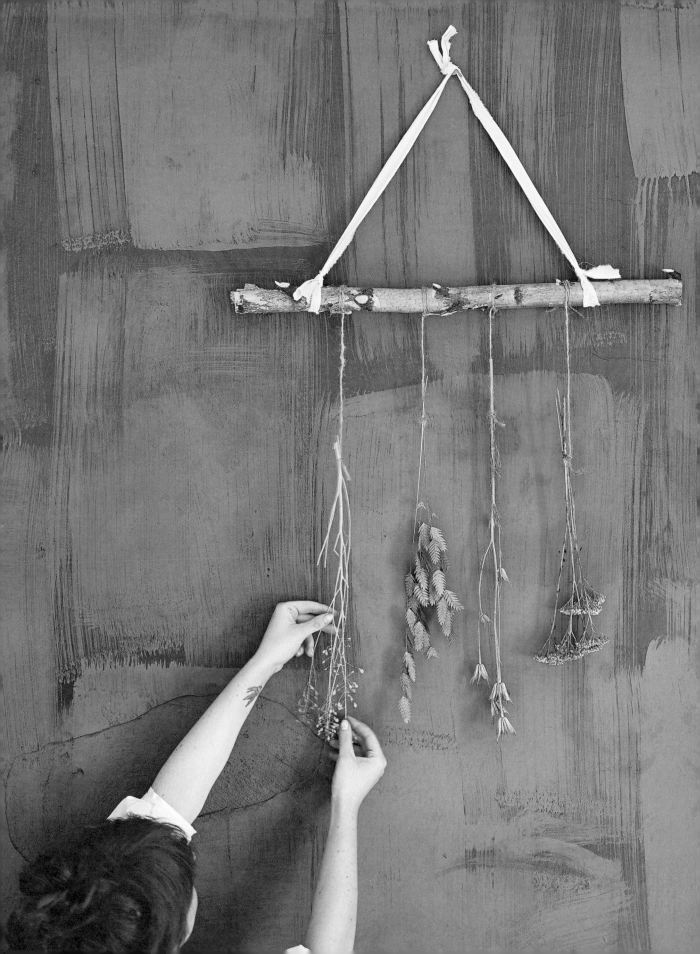

MATERIALS

1 beech branch, 60cm (2ft)
   in length
2 x 60cm (2ft) strips of calico
   fabric (about 3cm/just over
   1in wide)
Twine
Bonsai scissors or florist's scissors
1 small nail or picture hook,
   if required

FLOWERS + FOLIAGE

3 stems of dried achillea 'Parker's
   Variety'
3 dried nigella seed pods
3 stems of dried wild oat grass
3 stems of dried Northern sea oats

TIPS

▷ Be aware of balance: if you add something heavy on one side you will need to counterbalance it with an equal weight on the other side so that the branch sits straight and doesn't lean.

▷ On a larger scale, using one type of straight foliage such as ruscus on a much longer stick makes a lovely curtain-type installation that could form a really interesting backdrop for an event such as a wedding.

INSTRUCTIONS

1 First assemble all your materials. The stems can be any length you choose, we used stems that were between 30 and 40cm (12 and 16in) long. For the main branch, a small piece of wood that has fallen from a tree will work well; the thickness really doesn't matter as long it can take the weight of what you are hanging from it. Calico is not the only fabric you can use either: any material, rope, string or even ribbon will work just as well.

2 Start by attaching the fabric to the main branch. Tie a piece in a knot around each end, about 5cm (2in) from the end, and then tie the two strips together in a knot, being careful to keep the balance so that one piece is no longer than the other. At this stage, you might find it easier to hang the branch from a nail on the wall before you start adding the stems so that you can get a good idea of the shape of the hanging.

3 Next make little bunches of the stems you have chosen to use. Using 3–4 stems together creates a perfect bundle. You can keep the same materials together in bunches but feel free to mix them up. Wrap a piece of twine around the bundle of stems 3–4 times, approximately 5cm (2in) from the bottom. Hang the twine from the branch, wrapping it around the ends and tying the twine in a secure knot.

4 Space the bundles 5cm (2in) apart to ensure they don't become tangled. This will also keep the hanging looking simple and not too messy. Continue to add the bundles, attaching them at slightly different lengths if you wish to create an interesting shape. Finally, snip off any excess twine and hang the branch against a wall, door or from a hook in the ceiling.

Tropical wreath

SOMETHING A LITTLE MORE EXOTIC

A wreath can be much more than just a collection of flowers to mark a specific occasion. Who is to say that an unexpected and interestingly curated wreath isn't a work of art in itself? Something like this could happily take pride of place on a wall next to your paintings and other decorations.

When we're arranging, we love to take inspiration (and clippings!) from the world around us. But quite often we feel the need to include something a little more exotic to give the arrangement an interesting twist. The subtle colour changes and organic shapes of dried tropical leaves can be visually stunning and take arrangements in fun and bold new directions.

But tropical doesn't have to mean loud or garish. Here, we chose a colour scheme that sits well within the room and gives the whole piece a natural, subtle feel. We then accentuated this by using spray paints to apply light bursts of orange, brown and yellow to highlight these soft colour accents.

MATERIALS

Floral spray paint in terracotta, mustard, copper, white and cream
1 large clematis vine for the wreath base
Florist's scissors
Twine
Nail for hanging, if required

FLOWERS + FOLIAGE

40 dried palm leaves in various shapes and sizes

INSTRUCTIONS

1 As tropical leaves dry they develop slight variations in colour – some dry green while others dry brown. This wreath features a very subtle palette that goes from green to yellow to orange to white and then back to green. To make these changes more noticeable, you can use spray paint to enhance some of the natural hues of the dried leaves. First, put the leaves in groups of similar colours and then spray some of them a stronger tint to help create and enhance the tonal colour scheme you want to achieve. You can also use cream and white spray paints over stronger colours to create lighter shades. The aim is to keep everything feeling natural.

2 Make a basic vine wreath base (see page 18). Lay out all the leaves in front of you in the colour groupings you want the wreath to have. Add the two largest leaves to the wreath first and last, making sure there is a good mix of different-sized leaves going throughout your design.

3 Once you are happy with your arrangement of leaves and colours, start adding the leaves to the vine. You do not need a long stem to attach these leaves – the shorter the better as you need to keep the wreath as light as possible. Cut the stems so you have approximately 12.5cm (5in) of stem left.

4 The larger leaves help to give the wreath shape and provide a good base on which to attach the smaller leaves. Secure the first large leaf with twine on the top left-hand side of the wreath and angle it slightly to the left to give an interesting shape. If the leaf is heavy, you can secure it in a number of places. Tie on the other leaves arranged so that one colour blends into one another in a harmonious scheme; it may be necessary to spray some of them as you go along to create the desired blended effect. Tie the leaves very close together, nearly on top of one another; you need them to be clustered so that each leaf you add helps hide the tie from the previous one.

5 Add any delicate materials at the end so that there is less chance of them being damaged as you work. When you reach the point where you feel there are enough leaves, add the final large leaf that you have saved for the end. Tie this at the angle you think works best. If there are any strings that are hanging down snip them off.

TIPS

▷ Play around with colour in this type of creation. We once made a Matisse-inspired, block-coloured version of this wreath.

▷ Large wreaths can be really heavy, so make sure your wall fixing can support its weight.

Honesty mobile

INTRICATE DAINTINESS ON A BRANCH

We love dried *Lunaria annua* seed pods. Perhaps it's because when we were growing up our homes were full of them (gathering dust), but we also think their iridescent, pearl-like quality is so charming. In the language of flowers this pretty plant means virtuousness and sincerity, which is where it gets it common name, honesty.

This project is certainly not for the heavy-handed. It is delicate and intricate and is best hung where no breeze will cause it to tangle as it is almost impossible to disentangle the discs of honesty without damaging them. That being said, they look so beautiful hanging somewhere where they catch the light.

If you are lucky enough to have a little patch of land to grow plants, then be sure to sow the seeds from inside the discs. Although you will have to wait two years to reap the benefits, the purple flowers that appear are worth the wait, as are the seed pods that follow that you can use to create more mobiles. This is a project that keeps on giving.

MATERIALS

Bonsai scissors
1 natural branch (ours was
    70cm/28in long)
1 roll of clear thread (e.g. string
    for threading beads or thin
    fishing wire)
Screw hook for hanging, if required

FLOWERS + FOLIAGE

5 longs stems of dried honesty
    with seed pods

TIPS

▷ This mobile will hang nicely against
a wall from a nail, but looks even
better if hung from a hook or fixing
from the ceiling away from the wall.

▷ If you want to add colour to this
mobile, you can use spray paint
to create different coloured discs.
For one project we used sprays
in primary colours to make an
Alexander Calder-inspired mobile
to decorate a child's bedroom.

INSTRUCTIONS

1 Each long stem of honesty has approximately 5 smaller, more delicate stems growing from it. Snip off all of these smaller stems until the main stem is bare and then discard the stem. This project uses 25 smaller stems of honesty.

2 Strip the seed pods of their outer casing. On the side of each pearl-like disk there is a brownish or purplish covering containing the seeds that need to be removed. At the tip of each disk you will see a small spike, from here gently bend the disk to one side so that you can remove the outer layers. The iridescent disk underneath is very fragile and easily torn, so this needs to be done very gently. Set aside the small brown seeds to sow in the garden later.

3 Once you have prepared your stems of honesty as shown, it is time to get your branch ready to hang. Measure two identical pieces of clear thread and tie them securely to the two ends of the branch at equal points about 10cm (4in) from each end so that it will hang level (here the strings are 40cm/16in long). Tie up the two free ends in a secure knot at the top to create a triangle; this is the point from which the mobile will be suspended. Hang the branch where you want to display the mobile before attaching the individual honesty stems to it as this is the best way to avoid the threads becoming tangled.

4 Tie a piece of clear thread securely on the end of each section of honesty. Snip one end of the clear thread and leave a length at the other end long enough for it to hang from. The lengths need to vary so that they drop to different levels. Here the shortest length is 25cm (10in) and the longest 90cm (3ft).

5 As you attach the string to each stem, tie it securely from the branch, snipping away any excess string once the knot is tied. Start from one side of the branch, just inside the clear thread that is already attached from the fixing, and work your way across leaving about 2.5–5cm (1–2in) between each stem. Feel free to hang them at different lengths but make sure you balance the weight so it is not too heavy on one side. Here the longest piece is attached to one side with the next longest piece in the middle to help create a gentle shape (see photograph on page 144).

Kitchen herb bundles

CREATE A LOVELY HERBY SCENT IN YOUR HOME

This project would meet with William Morris's approval: it is both useful and beautiful. As well as looking good it also dries out herbs to cook with. And it doesn't just have to be made using herbs, it looks wonderful with flowers and all types of foliage that dry well. You can make it as a decoration at any time of year, using little pine bundles at Christmas, or brightly coloured leaves during autumn.

You can hang the bundles in front of a window or all around the kitchen walls. When bundles become too old you can snip them off and add new ones. They liven up a kitchen immediately as well as adding personality.

If you are picking herbs from the garden, try to gather them on a dry day, not after rain. As with flowers, they are best picked early in the morning when the sun has not had time to reach them, because as wonderful as the sun is, its heat will evaporate the essential oils needed to flavour your dishes or create a lovely scent in your home.

Choose different textures, colours and scents to make your bundles look and smell wonderful. As the herbs, flowers and leaves start to dry out they will lose their colour and start looking more brown, yellow and aged, which we think looks equally good. You can make this project as long or as short as you like.

MATERIALS

Florist's scissors
Twine
2 small nails or picture hooks,
   if required

FLOWERS + FOLIAGE

15 stems of bay leaf
15 stems of heather
15 stems of lavender
15 stems of black pepper
15 stems of rosemary
15 stems of sage
25 stems of thyme

INSTRUCTIONS

1 Before you start, lay out piles of the different herbs, flowers and foliage you will be using. Create bundles of the same herbs or create mixed bunches that complement each other.

2 Take 2–4 stems of each herb and arrange them into a small bundle. For this project the stem lengths vary between 10cm (4in) and 20cm (8in) long. It is more interesting visually when the stems are different lengths.

3 Decide where to wrap the twine on each bundle and strip all the foliage or flowers from that point downwards. If the twine is wrapped over the actual foliage it will encourage mould to form, which will spread down the stem. Wrap the twine around 4–5 times and then tie tightly. Snip off one end of the twine and leave the other end long enough so that it can hang off the twine that you will attach to the wall. Cut the stems so about 4cm (1½in) of it appears after the string.

4 Measure the length of the wall or window you would like to hang the herbs along. Allow for any sagging that may occur when you attach the herbs and cut the twine to length. If there are no existing fixings from which you can hang the twine, then a small hook or nail for each end will do. Attach the twine to the fixings quite tightly so that a natural curve is formed once the bundles are added. Start to add the bundles one by one so that they hang down approximately 5–10cm (2–4in) from the main twine. You can also hang them at different lengths if you prefer.

TIPS

▷ As well as removing foliage at the point the string is tied, be sure not to put too many stems together as this will encourage mould to grow between them. Air needs to circulate between the stems, so we would suggest no more than four stems per bundle, especially if you want to use them for cooking afterwards.

▷ Use different textures and colours each time you add a bundle so that it is interesting to look at and it draws the eye in.

Autumnal wreath

BARE AND BEAUTIFUL, TWIGGY BRANCHES CLINGING TO SUMMER'S LAST LEAF

Autumn is Katie's favourite time of year, and a wreath that truly embraces its season is something that we really love. As the colours around us change from greens to golds, and everything becomes decidedly crispier, nature provides us with a beautiful palette of burnt oranges, deep reds and rusty browns. Autumn is your chance to combine the beauty of the world outside with the flowers and foliage you've dried and preserved during the spring and summer months – the perfect ingredients for a vibrant autumnal wreath.

This wreath reflects autumn in all its sensibilities: its deep colours and crunchy textures; long walks through fallen leaves; bare and beautiful spiky branches clinging earnestly to summer's last leaf. The autumnal wreath can be hung anywhere in the home and looks particularly stunning when suspended over a fireplace.

MATERIALS

1 clematis vine for the
    wreath base
Florist's scissors
Twine
Strip of calico, 50cm (20in)
    in length
Nail for hanging

FLOWERS + FOLIAGE

4 preserved beech branches
    with leaves
10 stems of dried mixed grasses
1 stem of dried gypsophila
1 x 10cm (4in) vine of dried hops
1 stem of dried peppercorn,
    bleached white
1 dried poppy pod
2 stems preserved white ruscus
1 dried globe thistle

INSTRUCTIONS

1 Make a basic vine wreath base (see page 18). Cut your beech branches so they are roughly 50cm (20in) in length, grass stems to about 25cm (10in) and the rest of your stems to approximately 12.5cm (5in).

2 Start to add your materials to the vine. You can attach them while the wreath base is suspended, but we recommend to begin with the vine laid out on a table and add the final touches when it is hanging up. It is easier to add the larger, longer and leafier branches first; this provides a good base on which to add the rest. You can also make the overall shape that follows from the direction in which these branches are placed.

3 Tie your beech branches to the vine with twine. You will need to tie them in a few different places to ensure they are secure. Start by adding one branch to the top left and letting the natural shape flow out to the side. Then add a second branch to the bottom right, following the right-hand curve of the wreath.

4 Proceed to fill in between the two branches, leaving some of the vine base visible as a reminder of the naked autumnal branches on the trees outside. Start to add the other stems, setting aside the thin grasses and more delicate stems for later. The order in which these stems are added is up to you, but aim to keep an interesting mix of shapes and textures as you work around the vine. Make sure you spread out your autumnal leaves so that the colours of the wreath are balanced throughout: here, going clockwise, the colours radiate broadly from burnt orange, rusty brown, mahogany and pale yellow hops at the base, then rusty brown, burnt orange, mahogany, and finishing with a light clear gold.

5 Finally, add the thin grasses, hops and any other delicate materials that you have left over. These can be slotted in behind bigger stems; you may not need to tie them. Here, the hops are placed with the gypsophila at the base of the wreath to provide a soft focal point. The grasses make this wreath wilder and help to give it more shape. If you want a more compact wreath, trim the grasses to make them shorter. Once the wreath is complete, snip off any twine that may be out of place or looking messy. Use the strip of calico to make a tie around the top of your wreath and hang in position. You may want to add a few more stems when it is in place and this is the time to do so.

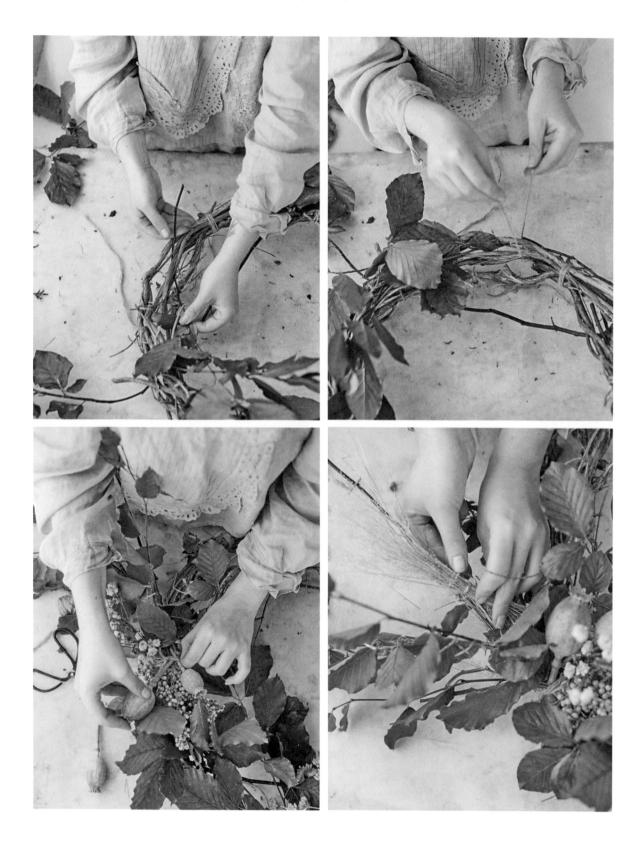

TIPS

▷ Time never stands still and autumn soon becomes winter. You can continually update this wreath with foragings and foliage found outside so that it will live on and always reflect the moment. A wonderful housewarming gift, the autumnal wreath can be a perpetual window to the outside world.

▷ If you decide to put this wreath on an external door, be aware that autumn can be windy. You may need to tie materials down more tightly. As grasses are delicate, you may need to use hardier materials.

Festive

SIX PROJECTS FOR
SEASON'S GREETINGS

Let your personality shine with a festive wreath of your own

For us Christmas starts in July as we begin to source Christmas trees and make wreaths for magazine shoots ahead of the winter issues, so by the end of December we have made a lot of Christmas wreaths.

Wreaths can be traced back to ancient times. In ancient Greece and Rome, they were a symbol of status and worn on the head, with materials such as laurel and ivy denoting different ranks or achievements. Harvest wreaths made with wheat or other grains were hung on the doors of homes as an offering in the hope of a good crop.

Christmas wreaths derive from Christianity and were traditionally placed on the door on the first Sunday of Advent. Table advent wreaths usually feature four candles representing the four Sundays of Advent, with a fifth in the centre

to symbolise Christ. These wreaths were made to represent hope and the circular shape was a symbol of everlasting life. Now they have become a popular symbol of Christmas and are a wonderfully bright reminder of the festive period as the days get shorter and the weather bleaker.

We often think that the wreath a person hangs on their front door during the festive season is a reflection of their personality and that, whether intentionally or not, they are saying, 'This is who lives here.' We love wandering around our neighbourhood, thinking about the personalities behind the wreaths we see, and it is always the homemade wreaths that catch our eye.

Any of the projects you see in this book can be made during the winter holiday just by adding in seasonal materials, such as holly, ivy, mistletoe, laurel or pine. Most of these are hardy and can withstand the effects of frosty weather.

Everything you have been drying during the previous months can also be used to make your Christmas wreath even more exciting and interesting. And don't be afraid to be creative with gold sprays, sparkles and ribbons. Foraging for Christmas materials can be great fun, but be sure to bring gloves if you are planning to pick some holly!

A homemade wreath is a wonderful thing to give as a gift. People really appreciate the time and effort you have taken to make something with your own hands, and having all your presents hanging on doors by early December could also save you any last-minute festive stress!

When you are making your own Christmas wreath, you might like to think about what you wish for your home and family in the coming year, and include flowers and foliage that symbolise those hopes and dreams (search on the Internet for the language of flowers for ideas). Making a wreath is also a really lovely project to do as a family, with everyone putting in something that they will be proud of when they come home each day during the festive season.

Giant pine wreath

THE ALTERNATIVE CHRISTMAS TREE

We live in the city, and as you might imagine our small apartments are already full of plants, so come Christmas time we just don't have enough room for a Christmas tree. However, we do have an alternative: a huge pine wreath. It still fills our homes with that evocative, festive scent and you can even decorate it with little fairy lights if you wish.

Pine lasts very well out of water, so if you put up the wreath in December it should easily last until Christmas. You can add other materials of your choice to make it special too: we added sticks we found in our local park, and holly and ivy from the garden to make it as full and festive as possible.

We use twine when fixing the frame as it makes it easier to add in smaller bits later by pulling them through the string. You could also use binding wire for this, but it will be harder to add to unless you use more wire. You can make a smaller version using the same steps to make a pine door wreath, but it is the scale of this wreath that makes it really exciting.

MATERIALS

1 willow vine 2m (6ft) in length
Twine
Florist's scissors
Large nail or hook for hanging,
    if required
Roll of binding wire (optional)

FLOWERS + FOLIAGE

4 x 15cm (8in) sprigs of holly
4 long stems of ivy
15 x 20cm (8in) pieces of cypress
    fronds or any other species of
    evergreen
15 x 20cm (6in) pieces of
    Scots pine
6 thin sticks foraged from the park,
    the wilder the better

TIPS

▷ This wreath can be quite heavy, so make sure that if it is hanging from a hook or a nail that it is secure on a wall that can take the weight.

▷ As you get nearer to Christmas you can add in some mistletoe – the white berries add something extra special to your wreath and it could come in useful should you have any special guests!

INSTRUCTIONS

1 Shape your willow into a wreath approximately 1m (3ft) in diameter (see page 18). You can work on it on a flat surface or on the floor, but it is better to hang it somewhere to work on that will be easy to access and will take a lot of weight.

2 Add the foliage so that it all faces in an anticlockwise direction. Start by adding a piece of cypress fronds into the bottom left corner, wrap a piece of twine around the end of the stem and the vine, and tie them tightly together. Next add a piece of Scots pine on top of the string you have just attached and tie the stem to the vine. Keep doing this all the way around the vine, alternating between cypress fronds and Scots pine if you are using both. This will provide a good base coverage.

3 At this stage the wreath will be looking quite neat and circular. If you would prefer it to look fuller and wilder, go around the circle again in the same direction as before. This time it won't be necessary to add more string as there is a good base already in place. Use your hands to find the string and weave in the new pieces of pine until they feel secure. If there is any string showing, you can simply pull out pieces of the pine to cover it. Making the wreath fuller at one particular point, such as the bottom right corner as seen here, will create a focal point and add flow to the wreath.

4 Now you can add all the little extras such as sprigs of holly and ivy at various points around the wreath; different colours and textures will give the finished wreath a more interesting look. Small fronds and foraged sticks can also add to the overall effect. Be sure to add any additional pieces in the same direction, so as not to disrupt the flow of the wreath.

5 When it is time to hang your wreath, you can simply suspend the vine itself on a large nail or hook, or you can add twine or wire to the top of the vine and use this to hang the wreath. You can also drape pieces of ivy on pegs or hooks nearby to enhance the natural feeling of the wreath.

Gift wrap mini wreath

GIVE YOUR GIFT A PERSONAL TOUCH

Sometimes it's hard to know how to give your festive gifts a personal touch, but these wreaths do just that. They add a little elegance and uniqueness to a gift and rather than being recycled with the rest of the Christmas wrapping, they can be hung on a window or door using the string from the rest of the parcel.

These small wreaths are not time-consuming to make, and also look really attractive as place settings at a dinner table, or hung with a ribbon from the backs of chairs – they could even be used as favours at a winter wedding.

These are great to make with family or friends as they are small and easy to put together. Here we have decorated them very simply, but you could make them as elaborate as you want. Add pine or ivy for a festive feel, or perhaps add a sprig of mistletoe if the recipient is someone special.

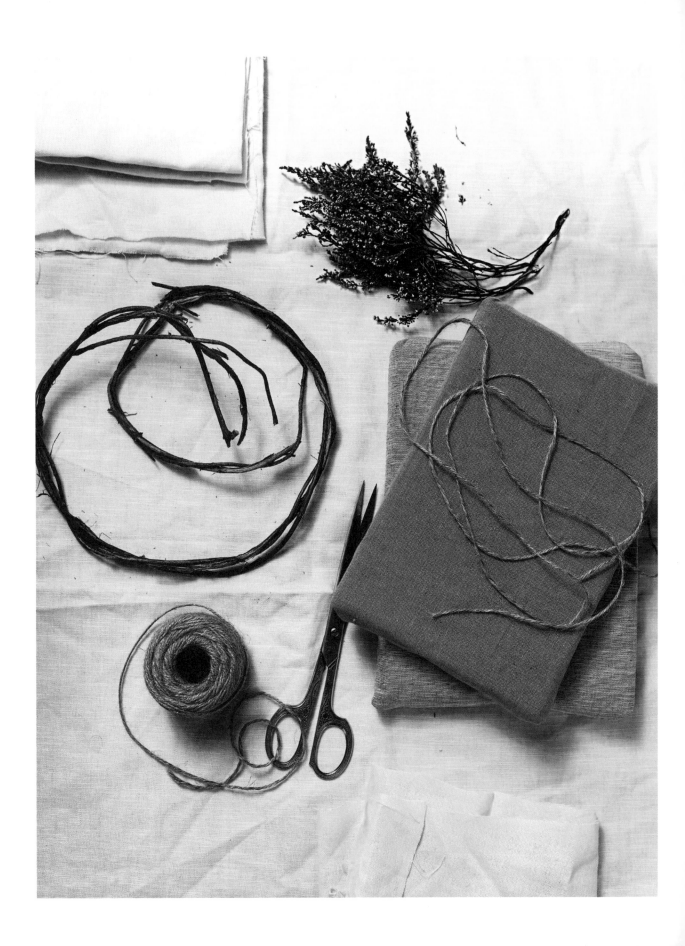

MATERIALS

1 piece of clematis vine, 50cm
 (20in) in length for the wreath
 base
Twine
Scissors

FLOWERS + FOLIAGE

5 stems of dried heather or other
 dried flower such as lavender or
 gypsophila

TIP

▷ We wrapped our gifts in Irish
linen that we buy from our local
haberdashery. Calico or kraft brown
paper also works well.

INSTRUCTIONS

1 Make a basic wreath (see page 18). For small wreaths it may not be necessary to tie the vines together as they may stay in a wreath shape naturally.

2 Cut the pieces of dried heather or other dried flowers into lengths of 10–12.5cm (4–5in) long.

3 Starting on one side, and working clockwise, feed the stems through the wreath structure – this should be tight enough to keep them in place.

4 Cut off any excess foliage from the back of the wreath that may be visible from the front when it is lying flat.

5 Using a piece of twine, weave it in and out of the wreath and around the wrapped gift.

Festive wreath factory

THE PERFECT FESTIVE PARTY DECORATIONS

The festive season is one of our busiest times of the year. During this period our studio is so packed with wreaths that it feels like we are working in a Christmas factory – we have to hang them from the ceiling, so we don't trip over them! While this is out of necessity, they always look so beautiful hanging together we think it creates a unique and interesting display.

If you have a large space as we do you can hang groups of large and small wreaths together. If you want to recreate this effect in your home but you have less room, you can make lots of small wreaths that you can hang together in groups. You could use them as festive party decorations and then give them to your guests as gifts when they go home.

If you want to make wreaths throughout the year, you can keep the bases that these ones are made on, and just change the materials you use. Either way this display is a wonderful way to show off all your different festive wreath ideas!

The instructions listed below apply to the 4 wreaths featured in this project. Simply refer to the materials list for what you will need to make any of the individual wreaths on the following pages. This is a project where you can get really creative – making them all, just making one or choosing a few to combine for a wall display.

INSTRUCTIONS

1 For each design you will need to use a vine base to create a basic wreath (see page 18). Some of the designs are simple, while others are a little more detailed.

2 Tie the materials onto the wreath base using twine. Each wreath should have a basic flow; this usually means that one side of the wreath is heavier with flowers and foliage than the other. For extra sparkle, lightly spray the flat pine with bronze or copper spray paint.

3 Once you are happy with the coverage you have on each wreath, plan where you will hang them. Attach lengths of twine or strips of linen to your wreaths to hang. The wreaths can be suspended from an existing beam (as in this case) but you can also hang them from hooks screwed into the ceiling or nails in the walls. If you have room you can hang them in a row, or in smaller spaces they can be hung in a group at different heights.

4 When they are all hung and you are happy with the placement, add any finishing touches: there may be a gap between two wreaths where you can place another branch, or you may want to add something eye-catching to enhance the overall design. For the simple olive and bronze wreath, we tied on a long piece of metallic bronze ribbon to finish.

Simple olive and bronze wreath

MATERIALS

1 clematis vine, 60cm (24in) in
    length for the wreath base
Twine
Florist's scissors
Floral spray paint in bronze
    or copper
2 x 1.5m (5ft) pieces of thinly
    cut linen
Metallic bronze ribbon, 1m
    (3ft) in length
Nails, or screw hooks for hanging
    from the ceiling, if required
Step ladder, if required

FLOWERS + FOLIAGE

3 wild nigella pods
4 small branches of cedar
4 branches of olive

Mimosa wreath

MATERIALS

1 clematis vine, 30cm (12in) in
   length for the wreath base
Twine
Florist's scissors
2 pieces of thinly cut linen,
   1.5m (5ft) in length

FLOWERS + FOLIAGE

3 stems of white limonium
4 stems of white mimosa foliage
2 stems or ruscus

Pine and ruscus wreath

MATERIALS

1 clematis vine, 45cm (16in) in
   length for the wreath base
Twine
Florist's scissors
2 pieces of thinly cut linen,
   1.5m (5ft) in length

FLOWERS + FOLIAGE

1 lichen branch
1 branch of Scots pine
7 small branches of cedar
2 stems of preserved white ruscus

Magnolia wreath

MATERIALS

1 clematis vine, 50cm (20in) in
   length for the wreath base
Twine
Florist's scissors
2 pieces of thinly cut linen,
   1.5m (5ft) in length

FLOWERS + FOLIAGE

1 stem of dried pressed fern
1 stem of dried honesty
3 short magnolia foliage
3 stems of green mimosa
5 small branches of cedar

From left to right:
Mimosa wreath, Pine and
ruscus wreath, Magnolia wreath

Festive Materials

THERE ARE MANY DIFFERENT MATERIALS YOU CAN USE TO MAKE YOUR FESTIVE WREATHS

You can take any of the projects in this book and adapt them to make them more festive. If you want to make a fresh wreath that will last more than a few hours then it's best to use a soaked floral foam ring. You can buy these in many different sizes.

This is the time of year where you can really get creative with coloured sprays too. Golds, silvers and coppers are traditional and can be subtle but feel free to get more colourful if you would like to create a more exciting wreath. Spray dried flowers, grasses, sticks, pine cones or tropical leaves to add an extra sparkle to your designs. Also feel free to embellish your wreaths with little props such as bells, bows, feathers or baubles, using wire or twine to attach them.

Festive wall hangers are also a great way of decorating your home if you have no room for a Christmas tree or if you would like to keep your wall decorations simple and natural.

There are a lot of different types of flowers and foliage you can use to make your Christmas wreaths – that's the magic of it! Here a list of some of our favourite materials, which will hopefully inspire you to get creative with your own.

FRESH

amaryllis
cupresus conifer
eryngium thistles
eucalyptus
hellebores
holly
ivy with berries
Japanese anemones
juniper berries
laurestine foliage
leather fern
majolica spray rose
mimosa foliage
mistletoe
moss
noble fir
olive foliage
pistachio foliage
poinsettia
ranunculus
rosehips
rosemary
Scots pine
sea-holly
silver fir
St. John's wort berries
wax flower
wild grasses
winterberry

DRIED

bay leaves
cinnamon sticks
cotton branches
dried eucalyptus
eucalyptus pods
fruit slices
gypsophila
hydrangea
lichen branches
limonium
nigella pods
palm fan leaves
pampas grass
peppercorns
pine cones
poppy pods
sea lavender
Spanish moss
willow branches

TIPS

▷ Using just green foliage can make a very eye-catching display.

▷ Wreaths become even more interesting when they are hung with different materials: linen, string and foil ribbon are all good options.

▷ You can add small fairy lights to your wreaths and use them as alternatives to a Christmas tree.

Latin Glossary

achillea 'Parker's Variety' *Achillea filipendulina 'Parker's Variety'*
achillea *Achillea spp.*
allium *Allium spp.*
amaryllis *Hippeastrum spp.*
anthurium *Anthurium spp.*
artichoke *Cynara scolymus*
basil *Ocimum basilicum NB*
bay *Laurus nobilis*
beech *Fagus ssp.*
blackberry *Rubus spp.*
cedar *Cedrus spp.*
clary sage *Salvia sclarea*
clematis *Clematis spp.*
common thistle *Cirsium vulgare*
common yarrow *Achillea millefolium*
coneflower *Echinacea spp.*
cosmos *Cosmos spp.*, chocolate cosmos *Cosmos atrosanguineus*, white cosmos *Cosmos bipinnatus 'Apollo White'*
cotoneaster *Cotoneaster spp.*
cotton *Gossypium spp.*
cow parsley *Anthriscus sylvestris*
cupresus conifer *Cupressaceae ssp.*
daffodil *Narcissus*
dahlia *Dahlia spp.*
delphinium *Delphinium spp.*
eucalyptus *Eucalyptus spp.*
fennel *Foeniculum vulgare*
fern *Dicksonia or Cyathea*
geranium *Pelargonium spp.*
globe thistle *Echinops bannaticus 'Taplow Blue'*
grevillea *Grevillea spp.*
gypsophila *Gypsophila spp.*
heather *Calluna vulgaris*

helenium *Helenium spp.*
helleborus *Helleborus spp.*
holly *Ilex aquifolium*
honesty *Lunaria annua*
hops *Humulus lupulus*
hydrangea *Hydrangea ssp.*
ivy *Hedera helix*
Japanese anemone, pink *Anemone hupehensis var. japonica*
jasmine *Jasminum spp.*
juniper *Juniperus spp.*
lady's mantle *Alchemilla mollis*
laurestine *Viburnum tinus*
lavender *Lavandula spp.*
leather fern *Rumohra adiantiformis*
lichen *Cotoneaster spp.*
limonium *Limonium platyphyllum*
lisianthus *Eustoma spp.*
magnolia *Magnolia spp.*
mimosa *Mimosa spp.*
mint *Mentha spicata*
mistletoe *Viscum album*
moss *Bryophyta spp.*
nigella *nigella spp.*
noble fir *Abies procera*
Northern sea oats *Chasmanthium latifolium*
olive *Olea europaea*
palm *Livistona spp.*
pampas grass *Cortaderia selloana*
pepper, black *Piper nigrum*
pistachio *Pistacia spp.*
pittosporum (variegated) *Pittosporum eugenioides 'Variegatum'*
poinsettia *Euphorbia pulcherrima*
poppy *Papaver rhoeas*

protea *Protea cynaroides*
ranunculus *Ranunculaceae spp.*
red-hot poker *Kniphofia spp.*
rose 'The Fairy' *Rosa 'The Fairy'*
rosehip *Rosa canina*
rosemary *Rosmarinus officinalis*
ruscus *Ruscus spp.*
sage *Salvia nemorosa 'Caradonna'*
scabiosa *Scabiosa spp.*
Scots pine *Pinus sylvestris*
sea-lavender *Limonium spp.*
sea-holly *Eryngium bourgatti 'Picos Blue'*
silver fir *Abies alba*
smoke bush *Cotinus spp.*
Spanish moss *Tillandsia usneoides*
strawflower *Helichrysum spp.*
St John's wort *Hypericum perforatum*
thyme *Thymus vulgaris*
wax flower *Chamelaucium spp.*
wheat *Triticum aestivum*
wild oat grass *Avena fatua*
willow *Salix alba*
winterberry *Ilex verticillata*

Suppliers

Listed below are all the suppliers we used in the making of this book. As we live in London we sourced all our flowers from New Covent Garden Flower Market: London, SW8 5BH | newcoventgardenmarket.com/flowers

However, don't despair if you live elsewhere as the internet is a wonderful place to search for your local flower market or florist and find the best blooms near you. Be sure to shop around for the freshest and best-quality stems. And don't forget to ask if you can't see what you want as most places would be happy to help and order in what you need.

For fresh flowers

Bloomfield Wholesale Florist Ltd
bloomfieldflowers.ie/about.html

Dennis Edwards flowers ltd
dennisedwardsflowersltd.com

DG Wholesale flowers
newcoventgardenmarket.com/wholesaler/
dg-wholesale-flowers-ltd

Pratley flowers and plants
newcoventgardenmarket.com/wholesaler/
pratley-flowers-and-plants-ltd

Zest flowers ltd
zestflowerslondon.com

For foliage;

GB Foliage ltd
gbflowers.co.uk/products/foliage.html

Porters foliage ltd
foliageshop.com

For fresh flowers farm grown

Flowers from the farm directory
flowersfromthefarm.co.uk

For sundries and supplies

Whittingtons sundries
whittingtons.biz

APAC
apacpackaging.com

Etsy
etsy.com

For ribbons

VV Rouleaux
vvrouleaux.com

Lancaster and Cornish
lancasterandcornish.com

For tapes (and other wonderful things)

Choosing keeping
choosingkeeping.com

J Glinert
jglinert.com

Present and Correct
presentandcorrect.com

For tools

Niwaki
niwaki.com/store/niwaki-garden-snips

For fabrics

The Cloth House
clothhouse.com

Woolcrest Textiles
6 Well St, London E9 7PX

This list again reflects the suppliers we used when making this book. But there are loads of great shops online that sell the materials and tools needed to create the projects in the book.

Index

Acknowledgements

Thanks to all our friends and family for being so supportive of us since starting a business and dealing with our constant absence yet ever present stress.

To Lorna and Dale and Sharon at Committee of Taste for ignoring the fact that we turn their shop into a flower factory as soon as they close the door every day and for being amazingly helpful and inspiring.

To Ian and his anthem van which we have hijacked many a morning and for always solving our problems when we find ourselves in a pickle and for always making us laugh and putting up with our terrible singing.

To Terry and all at Zest flowers for 5am fudge and saving flowers that look 'wormy'.

To Lee, Sam, John, Mick, Ron, Kim and all at Bloomfield for deciphering the names of the flowers we have made up and finding them for us always.

To Saul at Pratley's for welcoming us warmly from the very first day.

To Sonny and Eddie and all at Dennis Edwards.

To Dave, Tracey, Zak, Adil and all at GB foliage for always being lovely and sorting us out.

To Brian, Aaron, Russ and all at Porters.

To Holly at Rye London for use of her beautiful studio and Jane Cumberbatch for use of her wonderfully inspiring home.

To Aloha for being a wonderful assistant to Kristin and to us, now that we have forced her to believe that flowers are her thing.

To Joey for taking home plastic bags full of our leftovers and teaching us how she turns them into the most incredible cyanotypes you can see on page 10.

To Clare Lattin for all her nurturing, support and advice.

To Laura Jackson and Alice Levine for their support and encouragement from the very beginning.

To Momo for lending us the most beautiful pieces from her dreamy Momosan shop.

To Bauwerk Colour paints for sending the most beautiful paints we used as backdrops for the projects.

To Linda Berlin for finding us the most beautiful props in all of London.

To Harriet, Gemma, Helen, Tom, and all at Quadrille for putting their trust in us and for their guidance, knowledge and most of all patience during the whole book process, we are so grateful to have been given this amazing opportunity.

To Kristin Perers who is the most creatively inspiring human we have ever met. For all her assistance with the styling of this book. For taking photographs more beautiful than we ever could have imagined and literally changing the colours of the walls in her lovely home to match our arrangements (very Constance Spry). She let us take over her creative mind, her home and her dreamy flower factory studio to make this book a reality and she taught us a wealth of her knowledge throughout. Big thanks also to her wonderful husband William for welcoming us into his home and pretending not to notice the wall colours gradually changing.

To our families. Myra, Pat and Marg. Rita, George, Lucy and Marie. For always encouraging us to follow our dreams even when they took us on all sorts of pathways and for inspiring us with hard work, love and green fingers. We couldn't do any of this without your support.

To Mike and Paddy. For dealing with having part time partners since WORM began and for their constant encouragement, creative inspiration, love and continued patience. You are both wonderful.